Words Have Frozen Over

LES MOTS ONT GELÉ

Claude de Burine

Words Have Frozen Over

LES MOTS ONT GELÉ

☙

Translated by Martin Sorrell
Introduced by Susan Wicks

PUBLICATIONS
2001

Published by Arc Publications
Nanholme Mill, Shaw Wood Road
Todmorden, Lancs. OL14 6DA

Design by Tony Ward
Printed at Arc & Throstle Press
Nanholme Mill, Todmorden, Lancs.

ISBN 1 900072 50 5

The Publishers acknowledge financial assistance
from The Arts Council of England

For Claire

**Arc Publications: 'Visible Poets' Series
Editor: Jean Boase-Beier**

CONTENTS

SERIES EDITOR'S NOTE

There is a prevailing view of translated poetry, especially in England, which maintains that it should read as though it had originally been written in English. The books in the 'Visible Poets' series aim to challenge that view. They assume that the reader of poetry is by definition someone who wants to experience the strange, the unusual, the new, the foreign, someone who delights in the stretching and distortion of language which makes any poetry, translated or not, alive and distinctive. The translators of the poets in this series aim not to hide but to reveal the original, to make it visible and, in so doing, to render visible the translator's task, too. The reader is invited not only to experience the unique fusion of the creative talents of poet and translator embodied in the English poems in these collections, but also to speculate on the processes of their creation and so to gain a deeper understanding and enjoyment of both original and translated poems.

Jean Boase-Beier

Claude de Burine has been writing – almost entirely poetry, but some essays too – for well over forty years now. Her twelve volumes of poems to date all owe their existence, except the most recent, to a few small publishing houses. As is the case in the UK, these publishers work valiantly to gain and maintain a readership for fine poets who otherwise would remain unheard. Claude de Burine, rewarded over the decades with a number of significant prizes, but still relatively unknown in her own country, let alone elsewhere, has most recently been published by the prestigious, high-profile Gallimard, and it would be gratifying if she were now accorded the wide recognition her remarkable and distinctive voice deserves.

From her first volume, of 1957, to her last, 1997, Burine's subjects and content have altered little, but her attitudes and arguments slowly but perceptibly have. Though she divides her time between Paris and the spa town of Vichy, Burine is hardly an urban poet; rather, she draws inspiration and imagery from Nature, much of it the Nièvre landscape of central France, the region in which she grew up and which she knows best. Yet she is not principally a Nature poet either, if that term is taken to mean a focused meditation on the natural world, a way of letting Nature disclose itself and speak to us. To an extent, such revelations do occur in Burine's poetry, but as an incidental to something else. That something is the human dimension, an intense personal experience, sharp often to the point of pain, especially in the brittle domain of love. A great deal of Burine's poetry rehearses that experience, again and again, finding new ways of expressing it, the better to define it if not to secure it. The sense she gives is that certain enemies – not hers alone, everyone's – inevitably force open any grip we fancy we might have on love. The enemies are the obvious ones; illness, the passage of time, death. By her latest volume, *Le Pilleur d'Etoiles,* of 1997, it is hardly surprising that these dark, cloaked figures stalk nearly every page. In some remarks Burine has written about this collection, she alludes to a "mysterious, troubling presence in the fields, flowers, trees, countryfolk", the ghost in her poems. She indicates that she herself understands that presence no more than will we, the readers. Nevertheless, despite a growing distaste for the ways of the contemporary world, her faith in love, what she calls "passionate tenderness", endures. Burine's ambivalences, her hope vis-à-vis her pessimism, must be set against certain key experiences. She suffered serious illness some years ago, and has never fully recovered. Her health is troublesome, and she is obliged to lead a restricted and somewhat reclusive life as a result. On top of that, a number of her old and very dear friends have died in the fairly recent past, and this continues to be the cause of considerable grief. The themes, then, of her latest poems have to do with loss, while in earlier volumes love and thrilling desire were still presences.

Burine's growing concern with the fragile threads of love and life does not connote dark and morose poetry, quite the reverse. As Susan Wicks suggests in her Introduction, Burine's world dazzles, brought onto the page as it is by images which surprise and haunt us. Truth disclosed through astonishing images approximates Burine's poetry with Surrealism, and particularly with Eluard. There is in both the sense that powerful and troubling images invade our minds in order to tell us something vital; there is in both a certain formal elegance and concision which suggest an earlier period of love poetry. However, where Surrealism sees surprising images as unmediated truth – the real, the *sur*real beyond rationality, famously encapsulated in the definition of beauty as the encounter of an umbrella and a sewing-machine on an operating-table – Burine suggests something more metaphorical, as though images occurred not through any principle of random shock effects, but according to a hidden logic which will redefine what we think we know. The Surrealism of Eluard has always seemed closer to conventional metaphor than say, that of Breton or Desnos. For that reason, I would not want to suggest that Burine's affinities are with any Surrealist strand other than Eluard's.

If I have singled out Eluard, it is partly because it seems to me that the translation issues and problems which surround him are much the same for Burine. It is often claimed that Eluard is fiendishly difficult to translate. I hope it will be neither contentious nor platitudinous if I modify this and say that he is difficult to translate *well*. Arresting imagery surely is not of itself problematical if it is linguistically clear. The difficulty comes after translation, in the interpretation of images. For example, translating into *words* a bizarre dream usually is straightforward; understanding it is another matter. In that sense, I would contend that most, though not all, of Burine's imagery can be conveyed cogently from one language to another, assuming that the target language shares with French a reasonably similar cultural base (from French into English, and vice versa, is no great leap). However, when there are problems with Burine's images, they can be tricky and subtle indeed. As Susan Wicks has said to me, it can be difficult to know where one image ends and another begins, so seamlessly do they transmute. Punctuation seldom comes to the rescue, as Burine is sparing in her use of marks which delimit. Anyone who has read and tried to translate Apollinaire will know how stranded one can be when faced with no punctuation at all. Its lack, especially in Apollinaire's kind of free verse, has the effect of relaxing the boundaries of end-stopped lines, thereby creating new units of meaning through enjambement. In that, Burine and Apollinaire are not dissimilar. The latter, of course, saw his ambiguous syntax as part of a Cubist aesthetic of simultaneity. A given phrase may be, at one and the same time, the end of one sense group and the beginning of another. Although these ambivalences do occur in Burine's poems, thanks to her use of a free and loosely punctuated verse, she does not work according to an Apollinarian aesthetic. Rather, we get the sense that her images catch fire, then dissolve, like epiphanies, one after the other. The luminous image surely is the essential building-block of Burine's poetry; and, in the main, her lexical choices, syntactic development and intellectual arguments, in their straightforwardness, command less of the reader's and the translator's attention. The measure of her lines is created more by sense groups than by rules of metre. Thus, neither syllabic count nor rhyme has a particular place, and certainly not a privileged one, in Burine's craft. So, for example, in one poem (not given in this book), she can range from a two- to a twenty-one syllable line, while the poem as a whole remains well-controlled. Making the line subservient to a feeling, a thought, rather than the reverse, is perhaps an interesting characteristic of contemporary French poetry by women (though, of course, not exclusive to them), and is part of a certain ideology which seeks to reassert the primacy of individual experience localised in familiar places. The prevailing tendency, represented by such major figures as Bonnefoy, has been, on the contrary, to assimilate the particular and the personal into the general and universal. It may be that the directness of Burine's kind of individualised poetry, felt as much as it is thought out, and the push to abstraction of the Bonnefoy current, pose the translator challenges of distinct kinds.

Let me turn now to some short extracts from Burine's poetry, chosen for the problems they present the translator. I will focus on just two poems. The first is 'Mon été', from *L'Arbre aux Oiseaux*, of which this is the opening stanza:

> "Mon été étincelant et tendre
> C'était toi.
> Je te le donne
> Avec les tempes argentées du bouleau
> Le souffle d'or vieilli du tilleul
> Le chant du coq du coquelicot."

Clearly, there is no syllabic regularity; nor is there a rhyme scheme, even allowing for 1.4 and 6 (and for 'métro', in the next stanza). I know that some translators would say that this frequency of one vowel sound constitutes deliberate rhyme, but does it? As rhyming can be easily achieved in French, moments such as this surely are accidental, and without semantic force in the poem. Similarly, I can hear translators saying that 'été' in 1.1 and 'c'était' in 1.2 also constitute meaningful (if, strictly speaking, approximate) rhyme. Again, do they? Should a translation accommodate such coincidence of sound, or compensate for it? Surely not. The rhyme is accidental, of no consequence. Devoid of it, the two lines would lose no strength of meaning. Rather, what we find in this stanza is a cluster of single-line sense groups, each complete and discrete. The force of such splendid lines as 4 and 5 lies in the personification of the two trees named rather than in any heightened use of language organised on principles of metre and sound. The translator's obligation is to carry across that force, as clearly and tidily as the original. However – and this is one reason for my choice of this stanza as an example – the stanza's last line does contain repetition ('coq', 'coquelicot') which appears deliberate, and which lends it an ambiguity. Is the sense "the song of the cock AND of the poppy", as if there were a comma after 'coq'? Or is it "the poppy's cock-crow"? (If the latter, then of course it would have to be reworked, to avoid the unfortunate suggestion of 'poppycock'). I take Burine's line to be another of her potent images; the poppy is loud, shouting its redness, the way the red-combed cock crows. For that reason, I have opted for "The cock-crow of red poppies". But I have not found a way of rendering the sound repetition.

The final three lines of the same poem present another possible ambiguity, if of a different order:

> "Les bleuets ont allumé
> Leurs lampes tardives.

Bientôt, ce sera l'automne."

'Bleuets' is interesting. The obvious translation is 'cornflowers', which seems particularly appropriate, given the cornflower's luminous colour and circular shape, suggestive of a lamp, and given, too, that it blooms quite late in summer. However, according to certain respected dictionaries, the more normal spelling is 'bluet', and the first meaning given for 'bleuet' is 'kingfisher'. It could therefore be tempting to translate it thus in Burine's line. Such an analogy between a dazzling bird and incandescent light is original. It is similar to, but not the same as, Gerard Manley Hopkins's "As kingfishers catch fire, dragonflies draw flame..." But I have not found it possible to render neatly the ambiguity (probably unintentional) into English, and, with a certain sense of defeat, have settled for the more obvious choice of the two.

Let me offer a final example, this one the opening stanza of 'Sans toi', in *Le Pilleur d'Étoiles:*

"Sans toi,
Rien ne vient
Qu'une parole éteinte
Une peau
Qui ne vent plus prendre
Un feu
Sans victimes ni gloire"

Here is a stanza which illustrates my main points. The lines are short, pretty well end-stopped. Lexically and grammatically, they could scarcely be simpler. But, 'éteinte' and 'prendre' move us into subtle areas. First, adjectival 'éteint' can mean both 'extinguished' and 'faint', as of a sound or a colour. Then, 'prendre' might initially seem to attach itself to 'feu', and therefore to be translated as 'catch'. But, again, 'prendre' has another, intransitive meaning, 'take', as in 'take hold', 'set', or 'congeal'. I have discussed this stanza with Susan Wicks, who has made some valuable comments. I quote: "Because both these words have more than one meaning, I'm getting a sort of double image from this stanza. I get an extended image of fire, but I also get a more progressive image which moves from a general deadness or lack of light through the sense of a mask of skin to a burning at the stake..." So, for 'éteint', I have chosen 'lifeless', to combine 'dead' and 'dull'. The issue with 'prendre', though, is more delicate. Developing Susan Wicks's idea, the verb possibly controls a double meaning: looking forward to the next line, 'catch fire', and, looking back to the previous line, 'skin which does not take', in the sense of 'set' or 'bind'. This type of two-way syntax is reminiscent of Apollinaire's simultaneity. However, the most subtle part of Burine's stanza is the end, the last two lines. My initial reading was that, without 'you' (1.1), a fire will result, inevitably and regrettably creating victims and glory. But that reading was based on 'prendre' *only* as 'catch (a) fire'. So 'catch' had to yield, the more so as the French expression is 'prendre feu', without the indefinite article, as in English. Instead, 'take' gets the necessary ambiguity. Now, once the ambiguity of 'prendre' is established, and one imagines a comma after 'prendre', then the final two lines speak of a fire which will occur, but which will be pointless and inglorious without victims – in other words, the opposite of the first interpretation.

Lexical ambiguities of the kind found in 'Mon été'; syntactical doubling as in 'Sans toi', are relatively infrequent in Burine's work. To my mind, they constitute for the translator less what might be termed structural difficulty than local, itemised problems. Structurally difficult French poets would be, for example, Scève, Mallarmé, Ponge, Albiach. The difficulty in translating Burine's poetry is the going through the distillation process by which possibilities are tried until the purest solution is left (as perhaps it is in the case of Eluard). I suspect that it is easy to translate Burine adequately. To do better than that, however, is another matter. The differences between a poor, an acceptable, and an excellent translation of Claude de Burine are likely to be small, subtle – and crucial.

Claude de Burine at last is getting proper recognition in France. This very fine poet, this hope for a new, full-blooded and unsentimental lyricism in French poetry needs to be heard and attended to outside her own country.

Martin Sorrell, Exeter, 2001

I first met the poetry of Claude de Burine in Martin Sorrell's 1995 *Elles* anthology, a parallel-text selection which introduced seventeen more or less contemporary French women poets to a British readership. It seemed to me then that she was immediately noticeable as a French poet whose work *could readily be heard* by a foreign audience. The universality of her subjects, the simplicity of her language and unexpectedness of its relationships, all made her a prime candidate for translation. I'm sure I wasn't alone. And now Claude de Burine makes her real entrance, in a whole volume that combines poems from three of her most recent collections. Here her claims are even more obvious than they were.

"When I was little," she writes in a recent newspaper interview, "I must have been about five, one winter evening, I asked if I could go out. I left the warmth of the fireside and walked round the château, alone, in the cold and the dark. I wanted to bring back the moonlight in a champagne-bucket. I had to try and achieve the impossible. That was the night I became a poet." It's an uncompromising vision, a pure place as lost as Combray or the mysterious domain of *Le Grand Meaulnes*, and it makes for an intense, visionary poetry in a voice that is often fiercely despairing. It calls up quite naturally images that are as alive and luminous as the vision itself is bleak.

It's Claude de Burine's images that are the first thing that compels an English-speaking reader of these strange, passionate poems. Her poetry is a poetry built almost entirely on imagery, where metaphor is poetic structure, and the freedom of the vision itself becomes a source of meaning. The legacy of the Surrealists is immediately apparent. "It is pointless to fabricate the image. It comes to us as naked as unpainted wood, and as simple," as the poet herself puts it in 'All Souls 92' (in *Le Passager*, not included in this selection). And this primacy of the image can strike us oddly. Claude de Burine's metaphor-bank is a world we've come to regard as unreal, an archetypal natural world of seasons and snow and fire and flowers, an apparently naïve world which is in fact anything but naïve. Claude de Burine is a magician of the image: the silk handkerchiefs change colour even as we watch. And the sequence, however 'naked', is not, ultimately, haphazard and immaterial.

Still, the rural setting of many of these poems could present us with problems. The French apparently still have periwinkles and daffodils and snow and butterflies where we tend these days to have only embarrassment. You have to be a Louise Glück or a Michael Longley to be taken seriously about flowers. But in Claude de Burine's poetry the natural world is suddenly urgent, reactivated by its unexpected relationships. There is a paradoxical quality in these poems, a dance of meeting opposites, which makes even the most innocent metaphor deceptive and dangerous. Between the wine and walnut bed and marsh fires of 'I come back', it is the dead who must exhume the living, the dead who sit at table and eat and drink, who care if the bed still creaks – and the living who cry out for help, from their dark world underneath.

Those familiar with the French poetic tradition will not find themselves in entirely foreign territory. There seem to me to be echoes of Rimbaud in Claude de Burine's work, of Eluard and Duras. There is a poetic logic that uses symbol in a way that is not easily reducible, that at times succeeds in marrying the Surrealist's imaginative freedom with an earlier kind of rigour. Everything here is subtly mobile. Even the seasons somehow manage to tap into all the received connotations and yet make of them something we barely recognise – September the "strong wind", the lonely white horse standing between summer's clover and "the star of fur-skins"; summer a dry invitation to rivers of betrayal; autumn sexual love in every room of the castle; winter sexual renewal. Paradox is the medium Claude de Burine swims in. Between her fingers it is restless, full of colour and light.

At times we are confronted with a sensual experience that is almost impossibly rich. And Claude de Burine is certainly a 'rich' writer. As a poet, she has been prolific: there are twelve collections to date, a body of work from which Martin Sorrell has had to make difficult choices. In spite of a number of prizes won since her first collection, *Lettres à l'enfance*, was published in 1957, recognition and serious critical attention have come late. In the work itself, the themes darken: "Now I eat only stones. / Far off others pass / Like black boats." ('You: willows') The many-coloured fabric of desire is increasingly crossed by greyer threads of impotence and silence and loss.

But it is not only this combination of image and pattern that makes her poetry remarkable. It seems to me that against the background of current French poetry she is a rather lonely voice in another important way: while certainly not 'confessional' by any American or British definition, her poems do come with at least a suggestion of a recognisable human context. There is a decipherable human existence here, an existence which, over the whole spread of her poetic production, includes intimate relationships, childhood, aging, loss, Aids, the Nivernais landscape of her youth, the bars of the city, the town hall and poetic creation itself.

There are even poems in *L'Arbre aux Oiseaux* (1996) that read like a kind of desperate poetic manifesto. "They will claim: / What you write is nothing / Is the sleeping gong sounding / Deep in the deserted wood…" Martin Sorrell deserves all credit for first bringing this distinctive, erotic female voice to a British audience. This small but important selection is the tip of an iceberg. Unlike the ice-cube-dice of the chilling visitors of 'Is it your hand', it is full of words that "come to life", "dazzle like frost" and *stay*.

Susan Wicks, 2001

17

Words Have
Frozen Over
LES MOTS ONT GELÉ

DE «LE PASSAGER»

DÉPART

Il fallait sans doute
Que la pluie lave
A grande eau
Les tasses bleues du bonheur
Pour que tu prennes ces yeux sombres
Des cafés et des gares
Où l'absence
Est un ticket de neige,
Pour que j'accepte
D'abandonner ou de trahir
Les baies noires du lierre.

FROM 'THE PASSING TRAVELLER'

DEPARTURE

Quantities
Of rain no doubt
Were needed to wash
The blue cups of happiness
For your eyes to become the dark eyes
Of cafés and stations
Where absence
Is a ticket of snow,
For me to agree
To abandon or betray
The sombre berries of ivy.

TE SALUER

Te saluer
Comme on lance un bouquet d'œillets
L'été
Sur des dalles fraîches.

Prononcer ton nom
Comme on allume un feu
Dans une rue déserte.

Te toucher
Comme on touche le pain
Quand lui seul fait vivre.

GREET YOU

Greet you
The way carnations are thrown
In summer
On keen slabs.

Name you
The way a fire is lit
In an empty street.

Touch you
The way bread is touched
When it alone brings life.

L'ÉTÉ EST SEC

L'été est sec.
L'heure vient vite.
On brûlera bien encore ensemble,
Tu verras.

Tu auras tes yeux
D'où partent les bateaux
Qui mènent au carré vert
Là, où l'eau du fleuve doux
Te lèche mieux que moi.

Un soir
J'amènerai la boue,
J'amènerai le sang
Pour qu'elle ne puisse te toucher.

Ton sang peut-être, une nuit
Et le mien.

SUMMER IS DRY

Summer is dry.
The hour comes fast.
We'll go on burning well together,
You'll see.

You'll have your eyes
From which boats sail
Heading to the square green patch
Where the river's gentle waters
Lick you better than I.

One evening
I'll bring mud
I'll bring blood
So that it can't touch you.

Your blood perhaps, one night
And mine.

Ne joue pas aux dés,
Ce matin, avec le ciel,
Viens au château d'automne.
Dans chaque pièce
Pour la bénir
Je te ferai l'amour.

On enterrera la souris blanche,
Vêtus de noir comme la nuit,
Au fond du jardin
Sous le cassis,
L'amant des fortes odeurs
Et je t'offrirai la douceur
Du ventre nu
Des premières vendanges.

DON'T PLAY

Don't play dice
This morning with the sky,
Come to the autumn château.
In each room
To bless it
I'll make love to you.

Dressed in black like night,
We'll bury the white mouse
Deep in the garden
Under the currant-bush,
Lover of strong smells,
And I'll offer you the sweetness
Of a naked belly
Of the first harvest of wine.

LES HAIES SONT AU ROUGE

Les haies sont aux rouge.
La terre commence à fumer,
Les arbres à éclairer jaune.
Le soleil va se mettre au vert.

La Loire et ses sables
Gagnent tes yeux.
Je t'offrirai Paris,
Ville de l'encre et de l'or.

THE HEDGES ARE ON RED

The hedges are on red.
Earth begins to smoke,
Trees to shine yellow,
The sun to turn to green.

The Loire and its sands
Win your eyes.
I'll offer you Paris,
City of ink and of gold.

J'AI LONGTEMPS ÉCOUTÉ

J'ai longtemps écouté
Battre au loin
Le cœur bleu du froid
Lorsque j'habitais les maisons chaudes
Qu'on préparait
Les vins tourmentés des fêtes
Là-bas où tu vivais l'hiver.

J'avais laissé l'Automne,
Ses marins perdus,
Ses chemins où l'on voit surgir
L'homme à la cape sombre,
La femme au ver luisant.

Et je suis revenue pour toi, une nuit,
Tenter la chance,
Sous les étoiles fixes du givre.

FOR A LONG TIME

For a long time I've listened
To the blue heart of coldness
Beating in the distance
When I lived in warm houses
During the making
Of restless wines for festivals
In that place where you wintered.

I'd left behind Autumn,
Its lost mariners,
Its paths where suddenly one sees
The man in the dark cape,
The woman with the glow-worm.

And I came back for you one night,
To try my luck,
Under the fixed stars of frost.

PEUT-ÊTRE

Peut-être qu'en fermant les yeux,
En cueillant la pervenche à Noël,
En traitant la neige comme une princesse du sang,
Et les flammes comme les ambassadrices
Des longs manteaux pur les matins de brume
Retrouverai-je tes genoux, tes reins,
Ma bouche au creux de tes cuisses.

PERHAPS

Perhaps if I close my eyes,
If I pick the Christmas periwinkle,
If I treat the snow as Princess of the blood,
And flames the ambassadors
Of long coats for mornings of mist,
I'll discover once more your knees, your hips,
My mouth in the hollow of your thighs.

Un grand vent a pris soudain les fruits, les plantes, l'eau du bassin.
Seul le cheval blanc est resté debout.
Qui peut dire? Toi, le penseur aux glaieuls, hommes fiers s'il en est, hommes de courage, toi qui vas aux femmes comme on va au muguet.

La terre de chez moi a fondu: fleur de givre, tenue par des mains sévères.
J'ai voulu ta main dans ma main serrée, devant les Montagnes françaises, en face du Roi Mont-Blanc
Ou sous la petite cape vert-bronze des nuages en forêt du Morvan
Au bord d'un lac, aussi, j'aurais aimé, là où se noient les larmes, là où se pend le chagrin, où l'on mange le trèfle du souvenir, où l'on boit le soleil, l'été, avant l'adieu, quand on emporte la flamme pour l'hiver, pour les jours têtus de l'hiver avant l'étoile des fourrures.

T'entendre: le champ est encore vert, le bois profond.
J'avais le feu lorsque je touchais seulement ton doigt. Je filais la quenouille des perles.
Ta voix était ce voyageur qui frappe aux portes du soir.

A strong wind suddenly has caught the fruit, the plants, the water in the garden pond.
Now only the white horse stands.
Who can say? You , the thinking man with gladioli, proud men if ever there were, men of courage, you, the man who goes to women as one goes to lily of the valley.

The earth where I live has melted: frost flower, held in harsh hands.
I had wanted your hand held tight in my hand, in front of the Lord Mont-Blanc.
Or beneath the little bronze-green cloak of clouds on Morvan Forest
Beside a lake, I would have loved as well, where tears drown, where grief hangs itself, where the clover of memory is eaten, where the sun is drunk down, in summer, before farewell, when the flame is removed for winter, the headstrong days of winter before the star of fur-skins.

To hear you: the field is still green, the wood deep.
I had fire when merely I touched your finger. On the distaff, I spun pearls.
Your voice was the traveller who knocks at evening's door.

DERRIÈRE TES MOTS

Derrière tes mots,
Couraient les truites du langage.

Des gens allaient aux urnes,
Au chevreuil, aux finances,
A l'abreuvoir

Nous, nous faisons tomber la neige.
Avec les boules d'or, les feux prenaient bien.

L'automne remaillait plus loin ses rides.
Décembre allait venir.
Sa lumière couleur de menthe.
Ses lunes blanches, au bout des doigts.

BEHIND YOUR WORDS

Behind your words
Ran the trout-fish of language.

People on their way to vote,
To their venison, their financial affairs,
To their watering-holes.

Us: we made the snow fall.
With golden globes the fires drew well.

Further off autumn was darning its furrows.
December was coming,
Its mint-coloured light.
White moons at its fingertips.

TOI: LES SAULES

Toi: les saules
Toi: le canal
Toi: les sables de la Loire
Toi: le vent
Dans les chemins de boue
Où l'amour est encore plus fort
Parce que le cœur flambe.

Il fait gris.
Les arbres ont replié leurs ailes.
Les corbeaux font un sort aux prairies.
Les mots ont gelé.

Je ne mange plus que des pierres.
Les autres passent au loin
Comme des barques noires.

YOU: WILLOWS

You: willows
You: canal
You: sands of the Loire
You: wind
On mud paths
Where love's even stronger
Because the heart flames.

Grey light.
Trees have folded wing.
Crows cast spells on fields,
Words have frozen over.

Now I eat only stones.
Far off others pass
Like black boats.

LA MOUSSE

La mousse redevient la terre,
Comme la mer, la mer primitive.

Elles étaient belles, tes épaules,
Lorsqu'elles sortaient de la cuirasse brillante
Sous le panache blanc.

Elles sont belles, maintenant,
Quand le souvenir les découpe à vif
Sur le fond vert de l'île.

La Loire est un fleuve tranquille
Où ne s'arrête pas, la balance du Temps.

Près de toi, je fus celle
Qui cueillait les roses blanches des ruines
Te les offrait,
Lorsque le soleil avait poudré les tours.

MOSS

Moss becomes earth again,
Like the sea, the primitive sea.

They were beautiful, your shoulders,
Emerging from the brilliant breastplate
Beneath the white plume.

They're beautiful now,
When memory frets them raw
Against the green backcloth of the island.

The Loire's a quiet river
Where Time's pendulum won't stop.

Near you, I was the woman
Who gathered the white roses of ruins,
Offered you them,
When the sun had powdered the towers.

LES RÊVES

Les rêves qu'on enterre au fond des jardins
Là où les cyclamens fleurissent
Sont des enfants qui collent aux vitres
Leurs visages d'oiseaux blessés.

Ils regardent la table où le pain est dressé
Comme une nappe d'autel
Ou de noce avec le pavot noir
Le lit: ville interdite
Le fauteuil où leurs cuisses
Ne s'ouvriront pas sous la bouche fervente.

Ils sont les hôtes des murailles
Qu'assiègent les herbes,
Des plaines solitaires
Que seul visite l'oiseau des hautes tours,
Les marcheurs des fossés
Qu'éclairent les vers-luisants.
A peine une heure a duré leur vie
Le temps d'une caresse de l'amour.

Ils sont des papillons blancs
Qui se lèvent, ne vivent,
Qu'avec la mort.

DREAMS

Dreams we bury in the depth of gardens,
Where cyclamens flower,
Are children who press wounded
Faces against windows like birds.

They look at the table where bread is set
Like an altar cloth
Or a wedding-table cloth with black poppy.
The bed: forbidden city
The armchair, no thighs will open
There to the fervent mouth.

They are the high wall's guests
Walls besieged by grasses,
Solitary plains
Visited only by the bird of the tall towers,
Ditch-walkers
Lit by glow-worms.
Scarcely one hour their life has lasted,
The measure of a deep caress.

They are white butterflies
Which rise, which live
Only with death.

ELLE QUITTE LA MAISON

Elle quitte la maison
Où campent les livres,
Les poèmes, passagers clandestins.

Les fenêtres ferment
Parce que le soir est gris
Que l'absent tourne, dehors,
Pourrait entrer.

Elle le reconnaîtrait sous l'habit noir
Malgré la peau disparue
Elle n'aurait pas à l'approcher
Pour brûler comme une lampe.

Elle sait
Que les voitures s'arrêtent
Dans les bois silencieux
Avec les ceintures et les cordes
Quand les feux des prairies
Commencent à s'éteindre.

SHE LEAVES THE HOUSE

She leaves the house
Where books have made their camp,
Poems, stowaways.

The windows close
As the evening's grey,
The absentee's hovering outside
and might enter.

She'd know him under the black tunic
Despite the vanished skin.
She wouldn't have to bring him close
To burn like a lamp.

She knows
Cars stop
In silent woods
With belts and ropes
When meadow-fires
Begin to die.

JE N'OUBLIERAI JAMAIS

Je n'oublierai jamais que je t'ai perdu
Comme on perd son enfance
Une nuit où l'on ne'est pas sorti
Saluer la première neige qui tombe

Comme on perd sa jeunesse
Sous la bouche d'un passant

Sa vie quand on rencontre l'Écorcheur.

I SHALL NEVER FORGET

I shall never forget I have lost you
As we lose childhood
The night we don't go out
To greet the snow's first flurries.

As we lose youth
Against the mouth of a passer-by

Our life when we meet the Reaper.

JE VOUS AIMAIS

Je vous aimais
Comme on aime l'hiver
Venir le soir
Près des flammes heureuses.

Il est tard
Et les lampes se ferment.
La lune a plié bagage.

On entend le vent se lever
Faire son tour en ville.

La nuit sera noire.

I LOVED YOU

I loved you
As in winter one loves
Evening to come
Close to happy flames.

It is late
And lamps are closing.
The moon has packed its bags.

The sound of the wind rising
To make its rounds of the town.

The night will be black.

L'AUTRE MONDE

Comment dire
Ce qui fut silence
Portes fermées
Lampes éteintes?

Ce qui fut le feu
Sans le bois,
Sans la forêt
Pour filer la laine,
Sans la flamme
Pour les mains brûlées?

Et affirmer
Que tout se joua,
Là:
Le poème
Le chant
Le malheur?

Devint ce rien
Fait de rien
Qui sait,
Garde mémoire.

THE OTHER WORLD

How to say
What was silence
Closed doors
Extinguished lamps?

What was fire
Without wood,
Without forest
To spin wool,
Without flame
For burned hands?

And affirm
That all was played,
There:
Poem
Song
Unhappiness?

Became that nothing
Made of nothing
Which knows,
Keeps memory.

ET LE SOIR

Et le soir est tombé
Comme ça
Sans bruit
Comme un mouchoir brodé
Qu'on ramasse dans l'herbe.

A travers ta peau
Je voyais tes veines
Je suivais avec elles
Le chemin des jonquilles
Quand nous avions quinze ans
Dans les soirs doux et violents
Des bords de Loire
Qui sentent toujours le lilas et les saules.

Si tu vis encore de ma vie
Le printemps portera ton prénom.

AND EVENING

And evening has alighted
Like that
No noise
Like an embroidered handkerchief
Found in the grass.

Through your skin
I saw veins
I followed with them
The daffodil path
When we were fifteen
On the soft and violent evenings
Of the Loire's banks
Smelling always of lilac and willow.

If my life still makes you live
Spring will bear your name.

LES PLAGES

Les plages sont désertes
Les bateaux à l'arrêt
Devant les poissons
Qui passent au large.
Lorsque venait l'aubépine
Ou le magnolia,
Quand Paris dénudait ses épaules,
J'entendais ton rire.
La joie venait comme un moineau
Manger dans nos mains.

Je n'ai plus le bois pour flamber.
Je n'ai au doigt
Que la bague de fumée
De ton absence.

Nous nous retrouverons
Dans un temps bleu
Qui n'en finira pas d'agir.

THE BEACHES

The beaches are deserted
Boats stopped
Before the fish
Passing by out there.
When the hawthorn came,
The magnolia,
When Paris laid bare its shoulders,
I heard you laugh.
Joy came like a sparrow
To eat from our hands.

I've no more wood to burn.
The ring on my finger
Is the smoke
Of your absence.

We'll find each other again
In a blue time
Which won't be still.

DE «L'ARBRE AUX OISEAUX»

QUE RESTERA-T-IL?

Que restera-t-il de nous?
Une cigarette usée
Au coin d'un tabac,
Une attente
Sous les trois girouettes
Au fond d'une avenue,
Des pas secs et fiévreux d'été
Devant une mairie
Qui descend occuper la ville
Des pourparlers serrés, sévères,
Avec le gravier noir
Pour avoir ses aises, en bas?

La fumée bleue des campagnes
Ce ne sera pas nous,
Le Chrysanthème
Qu'on nomme: étoile des morts,
Ce ne sera pas nous
Mais peut-être ces pas, ces mains
Autour des vivants,
Cette inquiétude légère
Qui fait leurs yeux plus sombres
Leurs traits un peu tirés et leurs regards
Comme si
Derrière leurs feuilles
A la fin du dîner
Courait une épaule nue
Et blanche.

FROM 'THE BIRD-TREE'

WHAT WILL REMAIN?

What will remain of us?
A cigarette smoked
At some corner table,
A long wait
Beneath the three weathervanes
At the end of an avenue,
Sharp, fevered summer steps
In front of a town-hall
Descending to engage the town
In tough negotiations,
With the black gravel path
To unwind on, below?

The blue smoke of countryside
That won't be us,
The Chrysanthemum
Called the star of the dead,
That won't be us
But perhaps those steps, those hands
Around the living
That slight anxiety
Which darkens their eyes,
Strains their features a little and their gaze
As if
Behind their leaves
When dinner's finished
A naked white shoulder
Were gliding.

ASILE

Je ne suis pas morte!
J'entends le métro
Qui bout son linge
La toiture qui raconte
Les vents incertains.
J'ai l'œil aigu du brochet
La main vive du crabe
Et je serre les dents
Sur le morceau d'un pain blanc
Aux raisins d'orage
Que voudrait me disputer
Le jour.

ASYLUM

I'm not dead!
I can hear the metro
Boil its washing
The roofs telling
Uncertain winds.
My eye's sharp like a pike's
My hand's active like a crab's
And I sink my teeth
Into the morsel of white bread
Dotted with the currants of a storm,
Fighting off the challenge of the light
Of day.

Tu ne dois pas avoir peur
Même si le jour traîne encore dehors
Roule encore dehors
Heurte la vitre:
Ballon terni des dernières vacances.
Il parle avec ceux qui savent
C'est une affaire de gens qui savent
Ceux, tu vois bien,
Qui mettent les coudes à table
Rient rouge
Crachent cigares.

Ils font le feu des voyages
Raclent les miettes
Et bouclent la ceinture
Du dresseur de pierres.

Regarde l'agenda:
Il est en cuir
Son fermoir est doré
Souviens-toi avec lui
Du billard vert
Et du front vert
Des lampes autour.
Laisse-le faire
Il te prendra
T'emportera
L'allée est verte aussi
Et les arbres.

Un peu de parfum rôde
Il sent la femme
La lumière fine de ses jambes
Les chevaux perdus
Dans ses yeux,
Le vin qui plaisante
Quand ta peur file les laines bleues.

YOU MUSTN'T

You mustn't be scared
Even if day drags its heels outside
Still drifts outside
Bangs against the window:
Tarnished balloon of last holidays.
It speaks with those who know
Concerns people who know
Those, as you can see,
Who put their elbows on the table
Laugh red
Spit cigars.

Their journey-sparks fly
They stir up cumbs
And buckle the belt
Of the stone-mason.

Look at the diary:
Bound in leather
Its clasp is gold-plated
With it remember
The green billiard-table
And the green fringe
Of lamps around.
It will take you
Carry you off
The path is green as well
The trees too.

A stealth of scent
A woman's smell
The fine light of her legs
The horses lost
In her eyes,
The wine which make jokes
When your fright spins blue wool.

CES APPELS

Ces appels
Venus du fond des gares
J'ai peur
Je meurs debout
Sont des papillons
Noirs et or
Hôtes de la dernière nuit.

Le rail
Le bras arraché
De l'Automne qui rouille
Et se souvient
Des bois d'autrefois.
On achève les tables
Dehors
La lumière
A fini son temps.

THOSE CALLS

Those calls
Coming from inside stations
I'm scared
I'm dying on my feet
These are black and gold
Butterflies
Guests of the last night.

The rail
The arm torn out
Of Autumn rusting
And remembering
The woods that once were.
No more tables
Outside
Light
Has served its time.

JE M'EN REVIENS

Je m'en reviens tard
De chez les morts, ce soir.
Ils sont assis en rond
Boivent l'alcool blanc
Parlent
D'aller déterrer les vivants
Façon de voir
Si leur lit grince
Raconte encore
L'histoire du noyer.

Chez eux, la table est mise,
Le vin s'agite.
Nous ne sommes qu'une fumée grise
Un feu sur le marais qui tremble
Effeuille leurs pas
Lorsque nous appelons
Et qu'ils descendent.

I COME BACK

I come back late
From the dead, tonight.
They're seated in a circle
Drink white alcohol
Talk
Of going to exhume the living
So they can see
If their bed creaks
Still tells the tale
Of the walnut-tree.

The table's laid, in their world,
Wine stirs.
We are merely grey smoke
A fire on the trembling marsh
Plucks off their steps
When we call
And they descend.

EXISTAIS

Existais
Petitement
Dans mes petites demeures
Par temps de neige
A mots couverts:
Ici.

Les vis passer
Les bras, les jambes,
En haut,
La substance pensive.
Ces têtes fières
Allumées le matin
Et qui bloquent au vert.

Donnez-moi mes prairies
Mes bords d'eau
Leurs ventres d'alose et d'anguilles,
Les feux qu'on sème
Dans les jardins
Et qui prennent
Lorsque la nuit monte la côte.

EXISTED

Existed
In a small way
In my small abodes
In snowy weather
Of muffled words:
Here.

Saw them pass
Arms, legs
Up high,
Thinking matter.
Those proud heads
Lit up on mornings
Blocked at green.

Give me my meadows
My water's edges
Their bellies of shad-fish and eels,
The fires sown
In gardens
And which catch
When night climbs the slope.

JE ME PERDS

Je me perds
Dans tes yeux
Dans tes mains
Dans ta bouche
Je m'égare dans le champ
Quand le lièvre a passé
Dans les bois
Quand le cerf m'a couchée
Et j'explose
Contre la rosée métaphysique
Des murs.

I LOSE MYSELF

I lose myself
In your eyes
In your hands
In your mouth
I lose my way in the field
When the hare's gone
In the woods
When the stag's laid me down
And I burst
Against the metaphysical dew
Of walls.

IL Y A TON NOM

Il y a ton nom: mon village.
Il y a ta peau: ma ville.
Ton nom sur les arbres
Ta peau sur les arbres.

Si j'écris ta peau: je la touche.
Si j'écris ton nom: je le bois.
Si je suis la pierre: je suis ta route
Le sable: je suis ton chemin.

THERE'S YOUR NAME

There's your name: my village
There's your skin: my town.
Your name on the trees
Your skin on the trees.

If I write your skin: I touch it.
If I write your name: I drink it.
If I'm the stone: I follow your road.
Sand: I'm your path I follow.

ON DOIT SE TAIRE

On doit se taire
Laisser l'image se faner
Comme le gant blanc
Des noces avec la pluie
Ou bien s'éteindre
Et mourir rouge
Comme sa vie.
Les hommes bleus sont arrivés
Avec leur ventre qui sent l'ombre
L'aubépine franche
Les plaies qui s'ouvrent
Dans les maisons désertes.

WE MUST STAY SILENT

We must stay silent
Let the image fade
Like the white wedding
Glove in the rain
Or die out
Die red
Like life.
The blue men have arrived
With their bellies smelling of shadow
The frank hawthorn
The wounds which open
In deserted houses.

OÙ

Où
Dans quelle étoile
Va fleurir
La rose du sperme et du vent?
Quelle parole
Va naître d'elle?
Qui fermera
Les yeux noirs à jamais
De la mélancolie?

La lune est jaune
L'espoir est mort
La cloche d'argent et d'or
Qui scelle les unions fortes
Entre nous, n'a pas tinté
A peine un cil a-t-il bougé
Mais c'était les larmes

Le chemin existe pourtant,
Il est sûr,
Il ouvre au diamant
La main fermée.
Dans ce temps obscur du temps
Où le temps
N'a plus d'ombre.

WHERE

Where
In which star
Will flower
The rose of the sperm and the wind?
Which word
Will it engender?
Who will close
The eyes forever dark
With melancholy?

The moon is yellow
Hope dead
The gold and silver bell
Which seals the strong unions
Between us, hasn't rung
Scarcely has an eyelash moved
But it was tears

And yet the path exists
It is certain,
It opens the closed hand
To the diamond
In this dark time of time
Where time
Has a shadow no more.

MON ÉTÉ

Mon été étincelant et tendre
C'était toi.
Je te le donne
Avec les tempes argentées du bouleau
Le souffle d'or vieilli du tilleul
Le chant du coq du coquelicot.

Je te le donne
Avec l'odeur mâle du métro
Les statues des Tuileries
Qui s'endormaient pierres
Et se réveillaient femmes
Quand tu les berçais dans tes yeux.

Tout est dit, je crois,
A Paris et ailleurs
Et le monde n'a pas crié rouge
Lorsque tu as glissé, à l'aube.

Tout est calme, tu sais,
Et brûlant, comme toujours.

Tu retrouverais la barque
Et le silence
Et le couteau levé
La main qui claque
Comme toujours.
Les bleuets ont allumé
Leurs lampes tardives.
Bientôt, ce sera l'automne.

MY SUMMER

My sparkling and tender summer
Was you:
I give it you
With the birch-tree's silver temples
The lime-tree's breath of old gold
The cock-crow of red poppies.

I give it you
With the metro's male smell
The statues in the Tuileries
Which fell asleep as stone
And woke as women
When you swayed them in your eyes.

All I said, I think,
In Paris and elsewhere
And the world has not cried red
When you slipped, at dawn.

All is calm, you know,
And burning, as ever.

You would find again the boat
And silence
And the raised knife
The hand slapping
As ever.
The cornflowers have lit
Late lamps.
Soon, it will be autumn.

NE TE LÈVE PAS

Ne te lève pas
Reste sous la terre
Avec tes ors
Même si tes yeux
Même si ta bouche
Même si ton ventre
Se sont changés en terre
Avec la terre,
Ne te lève pas.

Tu portes au doigt
L'alliance des morts
Elle est faite de fumées
Du soupir des herbes
Avec le vent
Du cri blanc
Des oiseaux de la mer.

Aucune image n'a cours
Chez vous,
Aucun son
Vous vivez un temps
Sans prières ni larmes
Moi, je vis un temps jeune,
Debout
Dans l'odeur d'homme
Des aubépines
Moi je Te vis jeune,
Debout
Dans l'odeur des gares
Des squares
Du bar du crépuscule
Ouvert jusqu'au jour,
Qui ne se rend
Qu'avec le jour
Quand la nuit a flambé,

DON'T RISE

Don't rise
Stay below earth
With your gold
Even if your eyes
Even if your mouth
Even if your stomach
Have become earth
With the earth
Don't rise.

You wear on one finger
The wedding ring of the dead
Made of smoke
Grasses sighing
With the wind
Of the white call
Of seabirds.

No image is current
Where you are,
No sound
You are living a time
Without prayers, without tears
Me, I live a young time,
Standing
In the man-smell
Of hawthorn
Me, I live You young,
Standing
In the smell of stations
Squares
Nightfall bars
Open until dawn,
Which gives itself up
Only when day comes
After night has flared,

Laisse le râteau, la hache, la bêche,
Ce sont des armes à nous, vivants.
Tu es jeune dans ta peau
Jeune dans tes hanches
Et tes cuisses s'ouvrent
Lorsque ma main les ouvre.
Ta bouche a encore
Son cri de nacre
Et de sang frais.

Leave the rake, the axe, the spade,
These are the arms for us, the living
You're young in your skin
Young in your hips
And your thighs part
When my hand parts them.
Your mouth still has
Its pearl cry
Its cry of new blood.

MAIS QUAND J'AURAIS

Mais quand j'aurai fermé les yeux
Que vous serez sous les violettes
Ou les ronces comme moi
Que les nuages au-dessus de nous
Se feront se déferont comme nous,
Qui parlera pour nous?
Qui dira: «Toi, tes yeux,
Sont la couleur de la rêverie
Et des jeunes ardoises
Au printemps des pluies

Et toi: ta peau
Est la grive qui chante,
Tes mains sont ma chaleur
Et la fièvre de l'été
Qui porte ton nom».

Le temps va où il veut
Pose son habit de jonquilles
Et d'eau où il veut,
Nous n'avons rien
Qu'une aile de papillon qui sèche
Contre les vitres de la nuit.
Nous ne sommes rien qu'une poussière
Sous les lèvres avides du vent.
Seul le langage
Est le bronze qui dure.

BUT WHEN I HAVE

But when I have closed my eyes
When you lie beneath the violets
Or brambles like me
When the clouds above us
Will take shape and crumble like us,
Who will speak for us?
Who will say "You, your eyes
Are the colour of dreaming
And young slates
Which tile the Spring of rains.

And you: Your skin
Is the thrush singing,
Your hands my warmth
And summer's fever
Which bears your name."

Time goes where it will
Puts down its costume of jonquils
And water where it will,
We have nothing more
Than a butterfly wing drying
Against night's windows.
We are nothing more than a dust
Inside the avid lips of the wind.
Only language
Is lasting bronze.

TU NE VIENDRAS PLUS

Tu ne viendras plus à la table aux violettes
Tu ne boiras plus l'étang
Et l'on racontera ta vie
Avec le ton poli du meneur de chèvres.

YOU WON'T COME AGAIN

You won't come again to the table of violets
You won't drink again the pond
And your life will be told
In the goat-herd's polite tones.

UN JOUR

à Henri ESPINOUZE et Roland MASSOT

Un jour
Lorsque la pierre aura parlé
Le chêne
Dicté ses sentences
Une lumière inconnue
Mais blanche
Me conduira à vous.

De Perpignan, la catalane, où ils ont grandi, à Saint-Léger-des-Vignes, le Nivernais, mon village natal, où ils ont voulu dormir l'un près de l'autre.
A Henri Espinouze et Roland Massot, ces deux amis d'enfance, avec ma ferveur et mon estime.

IM Claude de Burine

ONE DAY

to Henri Espinouze and Roland Massot

One day
When stone has spoken
Oak
Laid down its sentences
A light unknown
But white
Will lead me to you.

From Catalan Perpignan, where they grew up, to Saint-Léger-des-Vignes of the Nièvre, village of my birth, where they wished to sleep, side by side.
To Henri Espinouze and Roland Massot, these childhood friends, with feeling and admiration.

IM Claude de Burine

DE «LE PILLEUR D'ÉTOILES»

LA VOYAGEUSE

Si l'on parle de moi,
Je me cacherais sous les violettes
Et deviendrai
Le scarabée d'or.

Si l'on me touche
Je serai la musique qui tourne
Au-dessus de vos saisons de Mai.

Si l'on m'aborde,
Je serai le feu.

FROM 'THE STAR-PLUNDERER'

WOMAN TRAVELLING

If I'm spoken of,
I'll hide under the violets
And become
The golden beetle.

If I'm touched,
I'll be the music whirling
Up above your Maytimes.

If I'm approached,
I'll be fire.

Et les heures maintenant qui éclatent comme des châtaignes, parce que la saison est froide, que l'absence aussi est froide et le regret.

Il fait soleil, parfois, dans le monde, on le sait.

Il y a des hommes qui vont et viennent, on le raconte, avec les termes de l'usage, montent les cubes étincelants.

Demain sera de glace sans doute: les boutiques du froid sont ouvertes.

On donnera à manger aux statues. À six heures les parcs seront fermés et la lumière saignée à blanc aux grilles de l'entrée.

And now the hours bursting like chestnuts, because the air is cold, absence as well is cold and regret.

Sometimes there's sun in the world, we know.

There are men who come and go, so it is said, in the appropriate language, fetching the dazzling cubes.

Tomorrow will be frozen no doubt: the shops of cold have opened.

The statues will be given food. At six o'clock, the parks will be closed and light will be bled at the gates.

Je ne suis pas d'ici.
Je ne tisse pas les fils
Des carrosseries brillantes,
Je suis assise
Dans l'évidence
De la terre aux oiseaux
Dans la pâte ancienne des saisons

Je descends de l'orge
Je descends du blé
De la grange
De l'ornière aux outrages
Du château
Qui s'offre aux usages

Je ne dis pas la ville
Où les têtes claquent au vent
Où la nacre vide loge le diamant

Voici qu'on est venu
Qu'on a trié les lentilles d'angoisse
Les prunelles bleues de froid
Qu'on a pris le Décembre en marche
Et qu'on les voit tourner,
Sous les lampes coupantes des avenues

La mousse, le genêt, la brume qui givre
Prennent leur place avec nous
Aux bars des carrefours

Les gants qu'on enfile
Ont la couleur du bouleau
Ses doigts
Sur une peau chaude

La rose, l'aubépine,
La feuille qui pourrit
Ont grandi avec nous
Joué avec nous
Dans les greniers

I'M NOT FROM HERE

I'm not from here.
I don't sew the threads
Of the brilliant coachwork,
I'm seated
In the truth
Of the bird-filled earth
In the old pastry of seasons.

I descend from barley
From wheat
The barn
The ravaged furrow
From the chateau
Inviting customs

I don't say the town
Where heads clack in the wind
Where empty oyster-shell houses diamonds

Here we are
We've sifted pain's lentil-lenses
The blue pupils of the cold
Caught in December on a walk
And we see them turning,
In the avenue's cutting lamps

The moss, the broom, the frosting mist
Take their place with us
In the corner bars

The gloves we slip on
Are the colour of birch
Its fingers
On warm skin

The rose, the hawthorn,
The rotting leaf
Have grown with us
Played with us
In lofts

93

Où les cuisses s'ouvrent
Lorsque la nuit regarde

Nous sommes avec elles, chez nous.
Les mots sont lents et brefs
Ils ont rôdé longtemps dehors.
Rentrent parce que le soir tombe.

La lune qui dort aux marais
A touché la poussière grise
Les yeux clos de ceux qui dorment
En bas.

Ils sont debout
Sans visage
Sans voix
Heure qui passe
S'effeuille
Porte leur blason sur l'eau,
Au fond des bois
Où ils s'attardent
Pour tuer encore
Lâcher leur mort sur nous.

Ils sont la neige,
Son rire blanc de vin nouveau
Le pétale de cerisier qui tombe
Sur nos épaules nues
Le foulard invisible du brouillard
Autour du cou de l'assassin
Et ses doigts de silence
Quand il dénoue, serre,
Pour l'hommage.

Le temps est ainsi
Pousse devant lui
Ses poissons morts
S'arrête un instant
Respire
Sur le banc de soleil et d'ombre
Qui sent le lièvre, le tilleul.

Where thighs part
When night looks

We're with them, at home.
Words are slow and brief
They've long prowled outside,
Come in now because night falls.

The moon asleep in marshes
Has touched the grey dust
The closed eyes of sleepers
Below.

They stand
Faceless
Voiceless
Passing hour
Sheds its leaves
Carries their painted shield on water,
To the depths of woods
Where they linger
Waiting to kill again
Let loose their death on us.

They are the snow,
Its white laughter of new wine
The cherry-petal falling
On our bare shoulders
The unseen scarf of fog
Round the killer's neck
And his fingers of silence
When he unties, squeezes
In homage.

Time is thus
Pushes in front
Its dead fish
Pauses a moment
Breathes
On the sun-lit shadowed bank
Which smells of hares, of lime.

LETTRE D'AUTOMNE

Le givre qui déjà fait ses pointes, les derniers soleils, leur tête penchée, flétrie comme ceux qui reviennent des vêpres, je voudrais te le dire, te dire aussi que la lune devient une orange lorsque le froid s'annonce, mais cela, tu le sais, ce sont des images de marché commun. Et c'est en cadeau que je te donne les petits feux dans les champs pour brûler les chaumes.

Ce ne sont pas des fleurs qu'on doit t'offrir mais les feux qui brûlent fort. S'allument ici, ailleurs. Tu les verras puisque je te les annonce.

Les heures qui courent en moutons dociles et sales n'ont pas la certitude des murs qui les abritent ni l'appui du béton-maire, ni de celles qui se voulaient des anges.

On commence à fermer les portes des granges sur des bois vivants.

Aux objets trouvés, on va chercher les mots des amours perdus.

Et c'est toi qui viendras m'attendre à cette gare où s'arrête et repart le train qui ne revient pas.

Frost dancing already on its toes, the last suns, head bowed, wilting like people coming home from church, this I want to tell you, tell you too that the moon becomes an orange when cold is around the corner, but you know it, these images are common currency. And it's as a present that I give you the little fires to burn off stubble in the fields.

Flowers shouldn't be offered you, but the bright-burning fires. Lit here, elsewhere. You'll see them because I'm voicing them to you.

The hours running like obedient and grubby sheep are not firm like the walls which shelter them nor the support of mayoral concrete, nor of those who wanted to be angels.

They're starting to close the barn-doors on living timber.

They're looking in lost property for the words of lost loves.

And it's you who will wait for me at that station where the train stops, leaves, and doesn't return.

JE NE PARLERAI PAS

Je ne parlerais pas
Avec le papillon
Ni avec la libellule
Ni même avec la fourmi.

J'ai rendez-vous, ce soir,
Avec le soir.
Ses gants de nuits blanches
Son visage d'épervier éteint.

I SHAN'T SPEAK

I shan't speak
With the butterfly
Nor the dragonfly
Nor even the ant.

I have a rendez-vous, this evening,
With evening.
Its sleepless nights' gloves
Its dead sparrow-hawk's face.

ÊTRE LÀ

Être là,
Te savoir, t'apprendre.
Savoir que je puis te coucher
Dans mes yeux,
Te coucher dans ma bouche,
Toi, debout,
Contre la table épaisse des saisons,
Moi, à genoux,
Sous les larmes amères de l'automne.

BE THERE

Be there,
Know you, learn you.
Know I can lay you down
In my eyes,
Lay you down in my mouth,
You, standing,
Against the solid table of seasons,
I, kneeling,
Under the bitter tears of autumn.

TU ES

Tu es ma lune d'hiver
Mon signe d'eau.
Envoie donc l'image faire les foins
Et saigne l'autre,
Son avenue qui roule ses arbres,
Ses mots qui crachent le feu.

YOU ARE

You are my winter moon
My water-sign.
So send the image to gather hay
And bleed the other,
Its avenue rolling its trees,
Its words spitting fire.

OÙ SONT MES HOMMES

Où sont mes hommes
De la nuit brillante?
Où est leur peau
Qui flambait juste?

Les mots sont las
Et leurs yeux sont éteints.
Il fait ce jour d'huître tiède
Où les mains sont fanées.

WHERE ARE MY MEN

Where are my men
Of brilliant night?
Where is their just
Flaring skin?

Words are weary
Their eyes lifeless.
It's a lukewarm-oyster day
A day of shrunken hands.

SI L'ON ME DISAIT

Si l'on me disait
Que tu es une lumière
Que tu es cette rose blanche
Que l'on met au cœur de l'hiver
Et que tes ongles sont la nacre
Qui brillent au fond des collèges
Où le lierre, le sapin,
Sont les enfants heureux
Qui gardent le froid bleu de la neige,
Je partirais.

IF I WERE TOLD

If I were told
You are a light
You are that white rose
Placed in the heart of winter
And your fingernails the oyster-pearl
Luminous in school corridors
Where ivy, fir,
Are the happy children
Keeping the snow's blue cold,
I'd leave.

J'AI LA RÉPONSE

J'ai la réponse du rosier
J'ai la réponse du chêne
Je suis dans l'intimité de l'herbe
J'ai table ouverte chez les pommes.
À quoi bon, la réponse haut perchée des villes?
Que voulez-vous que je dise au guéridon,
À son homme, qui tombent en transe,
Que j'avoue au pigeon
Qui tangue comme eux?

La réponse est là,
Dans la nervure du houx,
Dans ses décorations princières.

Si quelqu'un frappe
À l'heure où la vie est la vie,
La mort, la mort,
On le trouvera.

I'VE THE ROSE-BUSH'S REPLY

I've the rose-bush's reply
The reply of the oak
I'm deep inside the grass
Apples keep open house for me.
What use the town's reply, perched up high?
What can I possibly say to the table,
The man sitting there, both in a trance,
What confess to the pigeon
Pitching like them?

The reply is there,
In the holly's veins,
Its princely decorations.

If someone knocks
On the hour when life is life,
Death death,
He'll be found.

LES FLEURS

Les fleurs du chemin sont bleues
Comme les petites sœurs
Qui vont voir les mourants, la nuit.

Les nuages sont blancs,
Ce sont des chiens qui rêvent.

Le village est rouge.

C'est un pays.

Les fermes ont mis la veste de velours.
Tu respires, à peine.

THE FLOWERS

The flowers on the path are blue
Like the little sisters
Off to see the dying, by night.

The clouds are white,
Dogs dreaming.

The village is red.

It's a land.

The farms are wearing velvet coats.
You breathe, hardly.

SANS TOI

Sans toi,
Rien ne vient
Qu'une parole éteinte
Une peau
Qui ne veut plus prendre
Un feu
Sans victimes ni gloire

Viens
Que ce soit l'hiver.
L'hiver,
Où il me faut absolument t'avoir,
Où il me faut absolument t'ouvrir,
Où il me faut absolument te lire
Pour que s'écrive la légende.

L'été s'approche.
Pars, l'été,
Pars, dans les forêts noires
Où brillent encore
Les yeux sauvages de l'hiver
Là où je t'imagine le mieux,
Où je te vis le mieux
Pour m'endormir et manger ton visage
Poursuis et tue ce soleil à l'aube
Comme un papillon d'or.
Tue le soleil: ce tueur!
On nous dit: «écoute», on nous dit:
«Faites les rues,
Faites les tasses,
Partout et partout dans les villes,
Cherchez l'impossible amour,
Soyez ce mendiant du crépuscule
Qui lève la jupe blanche
Des petites filles
Ou la chemise déjà adulte
Des garçons aux yeux tristes
Des marins fous.»

WITHOUT YOU

Without you
Comes nothing
But lifeless speech
Skin
Which won't again take
Fire
Without victims or glory

Come
Let it be winter.
Winter,
When absolutely I must have you,
When absolutely I must ask you in,
When absolutely I must read you
So the legend can be written.

Summer's on its way.
Leave, in summer,
Leave, in the black forests
Where winter's wild eyes
Still shine
Where best I imagine you,
Where best I live you
To fall asleep and eat your face
Pursue and kill this sun at dawn
Like a golden butterfly.
Kill the sun: that killer!
We are told: "Listen", we are told
"Do the streets,
Do the cups,
Everywhere and everywhere in the towns,
Seek out impossible love,
Be that sunset beggar
Who lifts the white skirts
Of little girls
Or the already adult
Shirt of sad-eyed boys
Mad sailors."

On nous dit:
«Séchez les mots,
Qu'ils ne soient plus chair
Mais discours, mais sentences,
Guerriers qui tiennent les campagnes
Et la ville à l'heure.»
Quand il n'y a que le silence,
Et dans le silence,
Son bois de rossignols.

We are told
"Dry up words
So they're no longer flesh
But speeches, maxims, judgements,
Campaigning warriors in lands
In towns on the hour."
Let there be silence only,
And in the silence,
Its wood of nightingales.

VA

Va,
Empoisonneur des cadres
Rat d'usure,
Souris de placard,
Faisan des origines.

Laisse-nous ta dignité-bureau,
Ta pendule en bronze
Guillotine des heures
Et tes dossiers qui croulent
Bâtisseur de ruines.

Va
Porteur de chances
Faiseur de carrières à l'envers
Sous le caoutchouc de l'entrée
Et sa tête de moine aux outrages

Va
Le beau,
Parle bien,
Chien de falaises,
Pique-fleurs des églises.

Laisse-nous boire le sang de la terre
Le sang violent des morts.

Nous ne sommes que le vent
Qui pousse le navire.

                                        Le sida.

GO

Go,
Poisoner of plans
Extortionist rat,
Cupboard mouse,
Pheasant of origins.

Leave us your office dignity,
Your bronze clock
Time's guillotine
Your crumbling dossiers
You builder of ruins.

Go
Bearer of chances
Maker of back-to-front careers
Under the entrance's rubber
Its offending monk's head

Go
Handsome,
Speak well,
Cliff dog
Church-flower thief.

Leave us to drink earth's blood
The violent blood of the dead.

All we are is the wind
Pushing the ship.

                              AIDS.

Est-ce ta main de l'ombre
Que je touche
Ou ta main de vivant?

Je sens sur l'épaule
Son poids léger de jeune branche
Et j'entends bien ta voix qui parle
Beauté-Douceur
Des mots qui sentent le thé de Chine
Le sirop de framboises
Sous les tonnelles vertes
Les palais de marbre
Dont s'éprend la mer.

Qu'êtes-vous?
On voit que vous disposez des cubes invisibles
De petits dés
Dans lesquels l'eau gèle
De petits puits glacés
D'où naissent et partent
Vos mots de cristal.

Vous avez des manières blanches
Vos pas sur la neige
Sont des barques de silence qui glissent
Les lumières qui viennent avec vous
Ont l'éclat froid du givre.

Êtes-vous les ongles nacrés d'un dieu
Qui raie les vitres
Les soirs de fatigue?
Les inconnus dans la maison de Dieu
Qui savent comme lui
Renaissent comme lui
Se taisent comme lui
Attendent?

IS IT YOUR HAND

Is it your hand of shadow
I touch
Or your hand of life?

I feel on my shoulder
Its young branch's lack of weight
I hear clearly your voice speaking
Beauty-Sweet
Words scented like China tea
Raspberry syrup
In green tunnel-nets
Marble palaces
Which the sea falls for.

Who are you?
It's clear you have the unseen cubes at your disposal
Little dice
Where water freezes
Little frozen wells
Where your crystal words
Come to life and leave.

You have white manners
Your steps on the snow
Are boats of silence sliding
The lights which come with you
Dazzle like frost.

Are you the onyx nails of a god
Scoring window-panes
On evenings of fatigue?
Unknown people in God's house
Who like him know
Like him come to life again
Like him grow quiet
Wait?

Nul n'est venu jusqu'à nous
Pour nous dire,
Seul le chant du manteau
D'amandiers avec le vent
S'élève,
Retombe.

No one has come to us
To tell us,
Only the song of the almond-tree's
Cloak lifts
With the wind,
Settles again.

CLAUDE DE BURINE was born in 1931, at Saint-Léger-des-Vignes, in the Nièvre region of central France. A good part of her life has been spent in the region, which has always been a strong presence in the poetry she began to publish in 1957. To date, she has published some eleven volumes of poetry, as well as two prose works. For a while, Burine earned her living as a teacher. In recent years she has been dogged by poor health. She now divides her time between Paris and Vichy.

MARTIN SORRELL is Professor of French and Literary Translation, University of Exeter. Among his several publications, *Elles*, of 1995, a bilingual anthology of recent French poetry by women, first brought Claude de Burine to an English-language readership. His *Selected Verlaine* and *Collected Rimbaud* are published by OUP in its 'World's Classics' series. Sorrell has also written radio plays and stories for the BBC.

SUSAN WICKS' first collection of poems, *Singing Underwater* (1992) won the Aldeburgh Poetry Festival Prize. Her most recent, *The Clever Daughter* (1997), was a Poetry Book Society Choice and shortlisted for both T.S. Eliot and Forward Prizes. She has also published a short memoir, *Driving My Father*, and two novels. Now Lecturer in Creative Writing at the University of Kent at Canterbury, she lives in West Kent with her husband and younger daughter.

Also available from the
ARC PUBLICATIONS
Visible Poets Series
EDITOR: JEAN BOASE-BEIER

TADEUSZ RÓZEWICZ
(Poland)
recycling
TRANSLATED BY BARBARA PLEBANEK
AND TONY HOWARD
INTRODUCED BY ADAM CZERNIAWSKI

CEVAT ÇAPAN
(Turkey)
Where are you Susie Petschek?
TRANSLATED BY MICHAEL HULSE & CEVAT ÇAPAN
INTRODUCED BY A.S. BYATT

BARTOLO CATTAFI
(Italy)
Anthracite
TRANSLATED BY BRIAN COLE
INTRODUCED BY PETER DALE
PBS Translation Recommendation

MIKLÓS RADNÓTI
(Hungary)
Camp Notebook
TRANSLATED BY FRANCIS JONES
INTRODUCED BY GEORGE SZIRTES

MICHAEL STRUNGE
(Denmark)
A Virgin from a Chilly Decade
TRANSLATED BY BENTE ELSWORTH
INTRODUCED BY JOHN FLETCHER